# How Is Chocolate Made?

Angela Royston

Heinemann Library
Chicago, Illinois

Customer Service    888–454–2279

Visit our website at www.heinemannlibrary.com

Photo research by Melissa Allison and
Debra Weatherley
Designed by Jo Hinton-Malivoire and AMR
Printed and bound in China by South China Printing Company

09 08 07 06 05
10 9 8 7 6 5 4 3 2 1

**Library of Congress Cataloging-in-Publication Data**
Royston, Angela.
  How is chocolate made? / Angela Royston.
      p. cm. -- (How are things made?)
Includes bibliographical references and index.
   ISBN 1-4034-6641-6 (library binding - hardcover) -- ISBN
1-4034-6648-3 (pbk.)  1.  Confectionery--Juvenile literature. 2.
Chocolate--Juvenile literature.  I. Title. II. Series.
TX792.R69 2005
641.3'374--dc22

                                        2004018275

**Acknowledgments**
The author and publisher are grateful to the following for permission to reproduce copyright material: Art Directors and TRIP p.**13** (Mike Shirley); BCCCA p. **9**; Corbis Sygma pp.**6** (Annebicque Bernard), **17**, **18**, **19** (Richard Melloul); Corbis/Royalty-Free pp. **24**, **25**; Getty Images p.**12**; Getty Images pp. **28** (PhotoDisc), **28** (Stone); Green and Blacks p. **8**; Harcourt Education Ltd/Tudor Photography pp. **4**, **14**, **15**, **22**, **23**, **26**, **27**, **29**; Kim Naylor p. **7**; Science Photo Library pp.**11** (Mauro Fermariello), **16** (Rosenfeld Images Ltd), **20** (Tim Hazael); Still Pictures p.**10** (Ron Giling);TopFoto p. **21**.

Cover photograph of chocolate reproduced with permission of Harcourt Education Ltd/Tudor Photography.

Every effort has been made to contact copyright holders of any material reproduced in this book. Any omissions will be rectified in subsequent printings if notice is given to the publisher.

Some words are shown in bold, **like this.** You can find out what they mean by looking in the glossary.

# Contents

# What Is in Chocolate?

Most people enjoy eating chocolate. Chocolate contains some things that are good for your body, but eating too much chocolate can be unhealthy.

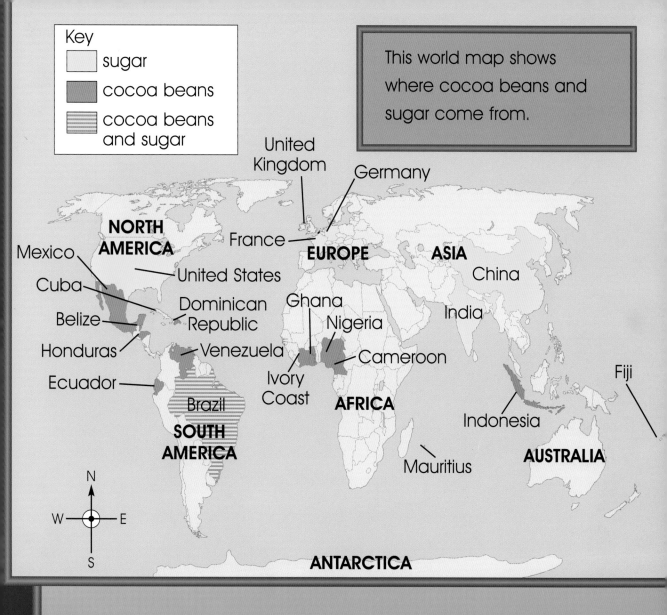

**Key**

- sugar
- cocoa beans
- cocoa beans and sugar

This world map shows where cocoa beans and sugar come from.

United Kingdom

Germany

NORTH AMERICA

Mexico

Cuba

Belize

Honduras

Ecuador

France

United States

Dominican Republic

Venezuela

Brazil

SOUTH AMERICA

EUROPE

Ghana

Nigeria

Ivory Coast

AFRICA

Mauritius

ASIA

China

India

Cameroon

Indonesia

AUSTRALIA

Fiji

ANTARCTICA

N
W — E
S

Chocolate is made from **cocoa beans**.

Chocolate also contains milk and sugar.

These **ingredients** come from many different parts of the world.

5

# Who Makes Chocolate Bars?

Several different **companies** make chocolate bars. Each company has one or more factories where the chocolate is made. Many people work for a chocolate company.

Some people work the machines in the chocolate factory. Other people pack the chocolate into boxes. Some make up names for the bars and **design** the wrappers.

This man's job is to check that the chocolate tastes good.

# Cocoa Beans

**Cocoa beans** grow in pods on cocoa trees. When the pods are **ripe**, the farmers cut them from the tree and take out the beans.

Workers spread out the beans in the sun to dry. They pack the dried beans into large bags. Then they send the beans to local companies. They send the beans to the chocolate **company**.

# Sugar

**Cocoa beans** are very bitter. Lots of sugar is needed to make the chocolate taste sweet. Sugar is made from stalks of **sugar cane** or from **sugar beets**.

These stalks of sugar cane are cut by workers in Brazil.

Sugar cane is fed into machines. The machines squeeze out the sugary juice. The juice is then boiled until it turns into small **crystals** of sugar.

# Milk

Cows make the milk that is used in chocolate. Milking machines remove the milk from the cows.

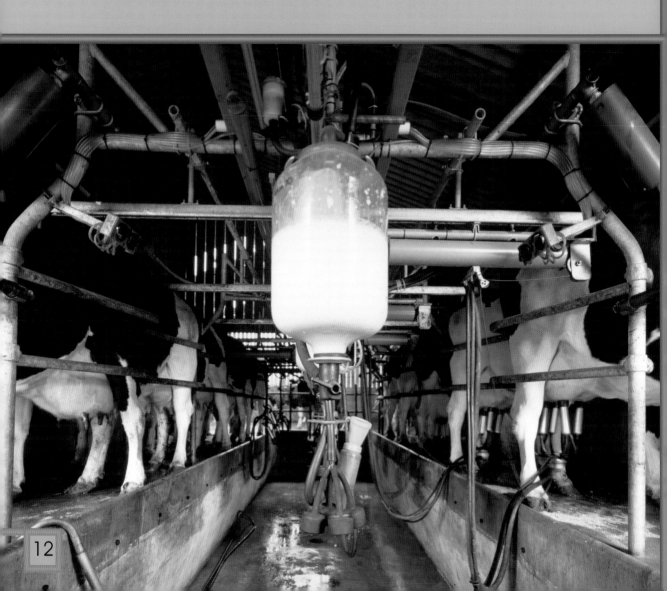

Once the milk is at the creamery, it is heated to kill any **germs**.

The milk is stored in a **refrigerator** tank. A milk tanker takes the milk to a **creamery**. A machine dries some of the milk.

# Other Ingredients

Many chocolate bars contain other **ingredients**. Flavorings, such as fruit and caramel, give some bars a particular taste.

peanuts

coconut

caramel

Peanuts, almonds, or other nuts are often mixed into the chocolate. Some chocolate bars are filled with coconut, puffed rice, or crunchy cookies.

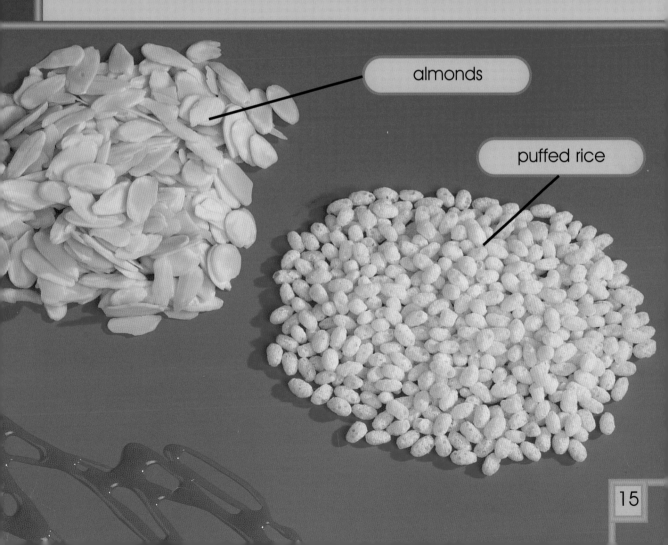

almonds

puffed rice

# Preparing the Cocoa Beans

Ships and trucks take **cocoa beans**, sugar,
and dried milk to the chocolate factory.
Here machines clean the cocoa beans.
They remove the shells.

The beans are slowly
roasted in a machine.

The ground beans turn into a solid called cocoa mass.

Workers feed the roasted beans into a machine called a grinder. It grinds the hot beans into small pieces. The ground beans are then cooled.

# Mixing in Sugar and Milk

Sugar and milk powder are mixed into the cocoa mass to make a soft dough. The dough moves through rollers. The rollers grind it into a fine powder.

The mixture is heated to change it into a liquid. The liquid is stirred for twelve hours.

The liquid now smells very chocolatey!

# Bars of Chocolate

While the chocolate mixture is still hot,
it is poured from the trough into **molds**.
Each mold is the shape of a single
chocolate bar.

These molds have **ridges** to divide the chocolate into chunks.

The molds move through a **refrigerator**.
As the chocolate cools, it changes into a
solid. Then the molds are removed. Now
you can see the bars of chocolate!

# Chocolate Wrappers

The bars of solid milk chocolate move along a **conveyor belt**. A machine puts a wrapper around each bar.

The wrapper keeps out the air and keeps the chocolate fresh.

The bars of chocolate are then packed into boxes. Each box contains the same kind of chocolate bar.

# Storing the Chocolate

Trucks take the boxes of chocolate bars to a **warehouse**. The warehouse is always kept at the same cool temperature. This keeps the chocolate from melting.

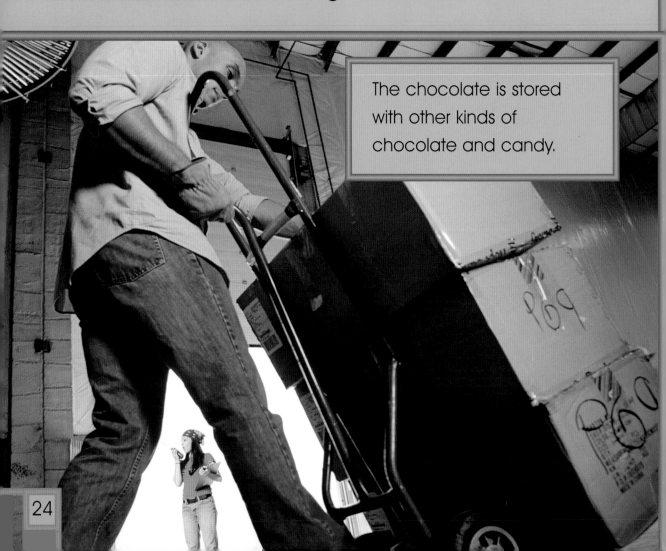

The chocolate is stored with other kinds of chocolate and candy.

24

When a store needs more chocolate bars to sell, they order them from the warehouse. A truck takes boxes of chocolate bars to the store.

# Selling the Chocolate Bars

Many types of stores sell chocolate bars. The store worker stacks them on shelves so that you can choose the kind of chocolate bar you want.

The store owner pays the chocolate **company** for the bars. The chocolate company uses the money to pay its workers, and to make more chocolate bars.

Some of the money you pay for a bar of chocolate goes to the chocolate company.

# From Start to Finish

**Cocoa beans** are cleaned, roasted, and ground.

Different cocoa ingredients are mixed with sugar and milk products.

The mixture is heated to make it liquid.

The liquid is poured into **molds** and cooled to make bars of chocolate.

# A Closer Look

A chocolate bar wrapper tells you the name of the bar, the **company** that made it, and the **ingredients**.

**STORE IN A COOL DRY PLACE**

Ingredients: sugar, Fairtrade cocoa butter, dried cream whole milk powder, Fairtade cocoa mass, cocoa mass, emulsifier: soya lecithin (non GM), real vanilla.
Cocoa solids: minimum 28%.
Milk solids: minimum 20%
Fairtrade ingredients 24%

MAY CONTAIN TRACES OF NUTS AND WHEAT

NUTRITION INFORMATION PER

| Energy | 2260kj/541kcal |
| Protein | 6.6g |
| Carbohydrate | 57.7g |
| Fat | 31.5g |

Ingredients

# Glossary

**bitter** not sweet

**cocoa bean** seed of the cocoa plant

**company** group of people who work together

**conveyor belt** machine that carries things on a long loop from one place to another

**creamery** factory that makes things from milk, such as butter, cheese, and powdered milk

**crystal** clear, solid piece

**design** decide how something will look

**germ** tiny living thing that can make you ill

**ingredients** things that are mixed together to make something

**mold** hollow container

**refrigerator** tank or large container that is kept cool

**ridge** narrow strip that is higher than the surface around it

**ripe** when seeds are ready to fall off the plant

**sugar beet** plant whose roots can be used to make sugar

**sugar cane** plant whose stem can be used to make sugar

**warehouse** building where things are stored

# More Books to Read

Burleigh, Robert. *Chocolate: Riches from the Rainforest*. New York: Harry N. Abrams, 2002.

Nelson, Robin. *From Cocoa Bean to Chocolate*. Minneapolis: Lerner, 2003.

Woods, Samuel, and Gale Zucker. *Chocolate: From Start to Finish*. Woodbridge, Conn.: Blackbirch, 1999.

# Index